# THE LAST DAYS OF IMMANUEL KANT

## THOMAS DE QUINCEY

FV ÉDITIONS

Kant

I take it for granted that every person of education will acknowledge some interest in the personal history of Immanuel Kant. A great man, though in an unpopular path, must always be an object of liberal curiosity. To suppose a reader thoroughly indifferent to Kant, is to suppose him thoroughly unintellectual; and, therefore, though in reality he should happen *not* to regard him with interest, it is one of the fictions of courtesy to presume that he does. On this principle I make no apology to the reader for detaining him upon a short sketch of Kant's life and domestic habits, drawn from the authentic records of his friends and pupils. It is true, that, without any illiberality on the part of the public in this country, the *works* of Kant are not regarded with the same interest which has gathered about his *name*; and this may be attributed to three causes—first, to the language in which they are written; secondly, to the supposed obscurity of the philosophy which they teach, whether intrinsic or due to Kant's particular mode of expounding it; thirdly, to the unpopularity of all speculative philosophy, no matter how treated, in a country where the structure and tendency of society impress upon the whole activities of the nation a direction exclusively practical. But, whatever may be the immediate fortunes of his writings, no man of enlightened curiosity will regard the author himself without something of a profounder interest. Measured by one test of power, viz., by the number of books written directly for or against himself, to say nothing of those which he has indirectly modified, there is no philosophic writer whatsoever, if we except Aristotle, who can pretend to approach Kant in the extent of the influence which he has exercised over the minds of men. Such being his claims upon our notice, I repeat that it is no more than a reasonable act of respect to the reader—to presume in him so much interest about Kant as will justify a sketch of his life.

Immanuel Kant, [1] the second of six children, was born at Königsberg, in Prussia, a city at that time containing about fifty thousand inhabitants, on the 22d of April, 1724. His parents were people of humble rank, and not rich even for their own station, but able (with some

2

assistance from a near relative, and a trifle in addition from a gentleman, who esteemed them for their piety and domestic virtues,) to give their son Immanuel a liberal education. He was sent when a child to a charity school; and, in the year 1732, removed to the Royal (or Frederician) Academy. Here he studied the Greek and Latin classics, and formed an intimacy with one of his schoolfellows, David Ruhnken, (afterwards so well known to scholars under his Latin name of Ruhn-ke-nius,) which lasted until the death of the latter. In 1737, Kant lost his mother, a woman of excellent character, and of accomplishments and knowledge beyond her rank, who contributed to the future eminence of her illustrious son by the direction which she gave to his youthful thoughts, and by the elevated morals to which she trained him. Kant never spoke of her to the end of his life without the utmost tenderness, and acknowledgment of his great obligations to her maternal care. In 1740, at Michælmas, he entered the University of Königsberg. In 1746, when about twenty-two years old, he printed his first work, upon a question partly mathematical and partly philosophic, viz., the valuation of living forces. The question had been first moved by Leibnitz, in opposition to the Cartesians, and was here finally settled, after having occupied most of the great mathematicians of Europe for more than half a century. It was dedicated to the King of Prussia, but never reached him— having, in fact, never been published. [2] From this time until 1770, he supported himself as a private tutor in different families, or by giving private lectures in Königsberg, especially to military men on the art of fortification. In 1770, he was appointed to the Chair of Mathematics, which he exchanged soon after for that of Logic and Metaphysics. On this occasion, he delivered an inaugural disputation—[*De Mundi Sensibilis atque Intelligibilis Forma et Principiis*]—which is remarkable for containing the first germs of the Transcendental Philosophy. In 1781, he published his great work, the *Critik der Reinen Vernunft,* or *Investigation of the Pure Reason.* On February 12, 1804, he died.

These are the great epochs of Kant's life. But his was a life remarkable not so much for its incidents, as for the purity and philosophic dignity of its daily tenor; and of this the best

4

impression will be obtained from Wasianski's account of his last years, checked and supported by the collateral testimonies of Jachmann, Rink, Borowski, and other biographers. We see him here struggling with the misery of decaying faculties, and with the pain, depression, and agitation of two different complaints, one affecting his stomach, and the other his head; over all which the benignity and nobility of his mind are seen victoriously eminent to the last. The principal defect of this and all other memoirs of Kant is, that they report too little of his conversation and opinions. And perhaps the reader will be disposed to complain, that some of the notices are too minute and circumstantial, so as to be at one time undignified, and at another unfeeling. As to the first objection, it may be answered, that biographical gossip of this sort, and ungentlemanly scrutiny into a man's private life, though not what a man of honor would choose to write, may be read without blame; and, where a great man is the subject, sometimes with advantage. With respect to the other objection, I know not how to excuse Mr. Wasianski for kneeling at the bed-side of his dying friend, to record, with the accuracy of a short-hand reporter, the last flutter of his pulse and the struggles of expiring nature, except by supposing that the idea of Kant, as a person belonging to all ages, in his mind transcended and extinguished the ordinary restraints of human sensibility, and that, under this impression, he gave *that* to his sense of a public duty which, it may be hoped, he would willingly have declined on the impulse of his private affections.

*The following paper on The Last Days of Kant, is gathered from the German of Wasianski, Jachmann, Borowski, and others.*

My knowledge of Professor Kant began long before the period to which this little memorial of him chiefly refers. In the year 1773, or 1774, I cannot exactly remember which, I attended his lectures. Afterwards, I acted as his amanuensis; and in that office was naturally brought into a closer connection with him than any other of his pupils; so that, without any request on my part, he granted me a general privilege of free admission to his class-room. In 1780 I took orders, and withdrew myself from all connection with the university. I still continued, however, to reside in Königsberg; but wholly forgotten, or wholly unnoticed at least, by Kant. Ten years afterwards, (that is to say, in 1790,) I met him by accident at a party given on occasion of the marriage of one of the professors. At table, Kant distributed his conversation and attentions pretty generally; but after the entertainment, when the company broke up into parties, he came and seated himself very obligingly by my side. I was at that time a florist—an amateur, I mean, from the passion I had for flowers; upon learning which, he talked of my favorite pursuit, and with very extensive information. In the course of our conversation, I was surprised to find that he was perfectly acquainted with all the circumstances of my situation. He reminded me of our previous connection; expressed his satisfaction at finding that I was happy; and was so good as to desire that, if my engagements allowed me, I would now and then come and dine with him. Soon after this, he rose to take his leave; and, as our road lay the same way, he proposed to me that I should accompany him home. I did so, and received an invitation for the next week, with a general invitation for every week after, and permission to name my own day. At first I was unable to explain the distinction with which Kant had treated me; and I conjectured that some obliging friend had spoken of me in his hearing, somewhat more advantageously than I could pretend to deserve; but more intimate experience has convinced me that he was in the habit of making continual inquiries after the welfare of his former pupils, and was heartily rejoiced to hear of their prosperity. So that it appeared I was wrong in thinking he had forgotten me.

This revival of my intimacy with Professor Kant, coincided pretty nearly, in point of time, with a complete change in his domestic arrangements. Up to this period it had been his custom to eat at a *table d'hôte*. But he now began to keep house himself, and every day invited two friends to dine with him, and upon any little festival from five to eight; for he was a punctual observer of Lord Chesterfield's rule —that his dinner party, himself included, should not fall below the number of the Graces

—nor exceed that of the Muses. In the whole economy of his household arrangements, and especially of his dinner parties, there was something peculiar and amusingly opposed to the usual conventional restraints of society; not, however, that there was any neglect of decorum, such as sometimes occurs in houses where there are no ladies to impress a better tone upon the manners. The invariable routine was this: The moment that dinner was ready, Lampe, the professor's old footman, stepped into the study with a certain measured air, and announced it. This summons was obeyed at the pace of double quick time—Kant talking all the way to the eating-room about the state of the weather [3]—a subject which he usually pursued during the earlier part of the dinner. Graver themes, such as the political events of the day, were never introduced before dinner, or at all in his study. The moment that Kant had taken his seat, and unfolded his napkin, he opened the business of dinner with a particular formula—'*Now, then, gentlemen!*' and the tone and air with which he uttered these words, proclaimed, in a way which nobody could mistake, relaxation from the toils of the morning, and determinate abandonment of himself to social enjoyment. The table was hospitably spread; three dishes, wine, &c., with a small second course, composed the dinner. Every person helped himself; and all delays of ceremony were so disagreeable to Kant, that he seldom failed to express his displeasure with anything of that sort, though not angrily. He was displeased also if people ate little; and treated it as affectation. The first man to help himself was in his eyes the politest guest; for so much the sooner came his own turn. For this hatred of delay, Kant had a special excuse, having always worked hard from an early hour in the morning, and eaten nothing until dinner. Hence it was, that in the latter period of his life, though less perhaps from actual hunger than from some uneasy sensation of habit or periodical irritation of stomach, he could hardly wait with patience for the arrival of the last person invited.

There was no friend of Kant's but considered the day on which he was to dine with him as a day of pleasure. Without giving himself the air of an instructor, Kant really was so in the very highest degree. The whole entertainment was seasoned with the overflow of his enlightened mind, poured out naturally and unaffectedly upon every topic, as the chances of conversation suggested it; and the time flew rapidly away, from one o'clock to four, five, or even later, profitably and delightfully. Kant tolerated no *calms*, which was the name he gave to the momentary pauses in conversation, or periods when its animation languished. Some means or other he always devised for restoring its tone of interest, in which he was much assisted by the tact with which he drew from every guest his peculiar tastes, or the particular direction of his pursuits; and on these, be they what they might, he was never unprepared to speak with knowledge, and the interest of an original observer. The local affairs of Königsberg must have been interesting indeed, before they could be allowed to occupy the attention at *his* table. And, what may seem still more singular, it was rarely or never that he directed the conversation to any branch of the philosophy founded by himself. Indeed he was perfectly free from the fault which besets so many *savans* and *literati*, of intolerance towards those whose pursuits had disqualified them for any particular sympathy with his own. His style of conversation was popular in the highest degree, and unscholastic; so much so, that any stranger who should have studied his works, and been unacquainted with his person, would have found it difficult to believe, that in this delightful companion he saw the profound author of the Transcendental Philosophy.

The subjects of conversation at Kant's table were drawn chiefly from natural philosophy, chemistry, meteorology, natural history, and above all, from politics. The news of the day, as reported in the public journals, was discussed with a peculiar vigilance of examination. With regard to any narrative that wanted dates of time and place, however otherwise plausible, he was uniformly an inexorable sceptic, and held it unworthy of repetition. So keen was his penetration into the interior of political events, and the secret policy under which they moved, that he talked rather with the authority of a diplomatic person who had access to cabinet intelligence, than as a simple spectator of the great scenes which were unfolding in Europe.

At the time of the French Revolution, he threw out many conjectures, and what were then accounted paradoxical anticipations, especially in regard to military operations, which were as punctually fulfilled as his own memorable conjecture in regard to the hiatus in the planetary system between Mars and Jupiter,[4] the entire confirmation of which he lived to witness on the discovery of Ceres by Piazzi, in Palermo, and of Pallas, by Dr. Olbers, at Bremen. These two discoveries, by the way, impressed him much; and they furnished a topic on which he always talked with pleasure; though, according to his usual modesty, he never said a word of his own sagacity in having upon *à priori* grounds shown the probability of such discoveries many years before.

It was not only in the character of a companion that Kant shone, but also as a most courteous and liberal host, who had no greater pleasure than in seeing his guests happy and jovial, and rising with exhilarated spirits from the mixed pleasures—intellectual and liberally sensual—of his Platonic banquets. Chiefly, perhaps, with a view to the sustaining of this tone of genial hilarity, he showed himself somewhat of an artist in the composition of his dinner parties. Two rules there were which he obviously observed, and I may say invariably: the first was, that the company should be miscellaneous; this for the sake of securing sufficient variety to the conversation: and accordingly his parties presented as much variety as the world of Königsberg afforded, being drawn from all the modes of life, men in office, professors, physicians, clergymen, and enlightened merchants. His second rule was, to have a due balance of *young* men, frequently of *very* young men, selected from the students of the university, in order to impress a movement of gaiety and juvenile playfulness on the conversation; an additional motive for which, as I have reason to believe, was, that in this way he withdrew his mind from the sadness which sometimes overshadowed it, for the early deaths of some young friends whom he loved.

And this leads me to mention a singular feature in Kant's way of expressing his sympathy with his friends in sickness. So long as the danger was imminent, he testified a restless anxiety, made perpetual inquiries, waited with patience for the crisis, and sometimes could not pursue his customary labors from agitation of mind. But no sooner was the patient's death announced, than he recovered his composure, and assumed an air of stern tranquillity—almost of indifference. The reason was, that he viewed life in general, and therefore, that particular affection of life which we call sickness, as a state of oscillation and perpetual change, between which and the fluctuating sympathies of hope and fear, there was a natural proportion that justified them to the reason; whereas death, as a permanent state that admitted of no *more* or *less*, that terminated all anxiety, and for ever extinguished the agitation of suspense, he would not allow to be fitted to any state of feeling, but one of the same enduring and unchanging character. However, all this philosophic heroism gave way on one occasion; for many persons will remember the tumultuous grief which he manifested upon the death of Mr. Ehrenboth, a young man of very fine understanding and extensive attainments, for whom he had the greatest affection. And naturally it happened, in so long a life as his, in spite of his provident rule for selecting his social companions as much as possible amongst the young, that he had to mourn for many a heavy loss that could never be supplied to him.

To return, however, to the course of his day, immediately after the termination of his dinner party, Kant walked out for exercise; but on this occasion he never took any companion, partly, perhaps, because he thought it right, after so much convivial and colloquial relaxation, to pursue his meditations,[5] and partly (as I happen to know) for a very peculiar reason, viz., that he wished to breathe exclusively through his nostrils, which he could not do if he were obliged continually to open his mouth in conversation. His reason for this was, that the atmospheric air, being thus carried round by a longer circuit, and reaching the lungs, therefore, in a state of less rawness, and at a temperature somewhat higher, would be less apt to irritate them. By a steady perseverance in this practice, which he constantly recommended to his friends, he flattered himself with a long immunity from coughs, colds, hoarseness, and every mode of defluxion; and the fact really was, that these troublesome affections attacked him very rarely. Indeed I myself, by only occasionally adopting his rule, have found my chest not so liable as formerly to such attacks.

At six o'clock he sat down to his library table, which was a plain ordinary piece of furniture, and read till dusk. During this period of dubious light, so friendly to thought, he rested in tranquil meditation on what he had been reading, provided the book were worth it; if not, he sketched his lecture for the next day, or some part of any book he might then be composing. During this state of repose he took his station winter and summer by the stove, looking through the window at the old tower of Lobenicht; not that he could be said properly to see it, but the tower rested upon his eye, — obscurely, or but half revealed to his consciousness. No words seemed forcible enough to express his sense of the gratification which he derived from this old tower, when seen under these circumstances of twilight and quiet reverie. The sequel, indeed, showed how important it was to his comfort; for at length some poplars in a neighboring garden shot up to such a height as to obscure the tower, upon which Kant became very uneasy and restless, and at length found himself positively unable to pursue his evening meditations. Fortunately, the proprietor of the garden was a very considerate and obliging person, who had, besides, a high regard for Kant; and, accordingly, upon a representation of the case being made to him, he gave orders that the poplars should be cropped. This was done, the old tower of Lobenicht was again unveiled, and Kant recovered his equanimity, and pursued his twilight meditations as before.

After the candles were brought, Kant prosecuted his studies till nearly ten o'clock. A quarter of an hour before retiring for the night, he withdrew his mind as much as possible from every class of thoughts which demanded any exertion or energy of attention, on the principle, that by stimulating and exciting him too much, such thoughts would be apt to cause wakefulness; and the slightest interference with his customary hour of falling asleep, was in the highest degree unpleasant to him. Happily, this was with him a very rare occurrence.

He undressed himself without his servant's assistance, but in such an order, and with such a Roman regard to decorum and the *to prepon*, that he was always ready at a moment's warning to make his appearance without embarrassment to himself or to others. This done, he lay down on a mattress, and wrapped himself up in a quilt, which in summer was always of cotton,— in autumn, of wool; at the setting-in of winter he used both—and against very severe cold, he protected himself by one of eider-down, of which the part which covered his shoulders was not stuffed with feathers, but padded, or rather wadded closely with layers of wool. Long practice had taught him a very dexterous mode of *nesting* himself, as it were, in the bed-clothes. First of all, he sat down on the bedside; then with an agile motion he vaulted obliquely into his lair; next he drew one corner of the bedclothes under his left shoulder, and passing it below his back, brought it round so as to rest under his right shoulder; fourthly, by a particular *tour d'adresse*, he treated the other corner in the same way, and finally contrived to roll it round his whole person. Thus swathed like a mummy, or (as I used to tell him) self- involved like the silk-worm in its cocoon, he awaited the approach of sleep, which generally came on immediately. For Kant's health was exquisite; not mere negative health, or the absence of pain, but a state of positive pleasurable sensation, and a genial sense of the entire possession of all his activities. Accordingly, when packed up for the night in the way I have described, he would often ejaculate to himself (as he used to tell us at dinner) —'Is it possible to conceive a human being with more perfect health than myself?' In fact, such was the innocence of his life, and such the happy condition of his situation, that no uneasy passion ever arose to excite him— nor care to harass—nor pain to awake him. Even in the severest winter his sleeping-room was without a fire; only in his latter years he yielded so far to the entreaties of his friends as to allow of a very small one. All nursing or self-indulgence found no quarter with Kant. In fact, five minutes, in the coldest weather, sufficed to supersede the first chill of the bed, by the diffusion of a general glow over his person. If he had any occasion to leave his room in the night-time, (for it was always kept dark day and night, summer and winter,) he guided himself by a rope, which was duly attached to his bed-post every night, and carried into the adjoining apartment.

Kant never perspired, [6] night or day. Yet it was astonishing how much heat he supported habitually in his study, and in fact was not easy if it wanted but one degree of this heat. Seventy-five degrees of Fahrenheit was the invariable temperature of this room in which he chiefly lived; and if it fell below that point, no matter at what season of the year, he had it raised artificially to the usual standard. In the heats of summer he went thinly dressed, and invariably in silk stockings; yet, as even this dress could not always secure him against perspiring when engaged in active exercise, he had a singular remedy in reserve. Retiring to some shady place, he stood still and motionless—with the air and attitude of a person listening, or in suspense— until his usual *aridity* was restored. Even in the most sultry summer night, if the slightest trace of perspiration had sullied his night-dress, he spoke of it with emphasis, as of an accident that perfectly shocked him.

On this occasion, whilst illustrating Kant's notions of the animal economy, it may be as well to add one other particular, which is, that for fear of obstructing the circulation of the blood, he never would wear garters; yet, as he found it difficult to keep up his stockings without them, he had invented for himself a most elaborate substitute, which I shall describe. In a little pocket, somewhat smaller than a watch-pocket, but occupying pretty nearly the same situation as a watch-pocket on each thigh, there was placed a small box, something like a watch-case, but smaller; into this box was introduced a watch-spring in a wheel, round about which wheel was wound an elastic cord, for regulating the force of which there was a separate contrivance. To the two ends of this cord were attached hooks, which hooks were carried through a small aperture in the pockets, and so passing down the inner and the outer side of the thigh, caught hold of two loops which were fixed on the off side and the near side of each stocking. As might be expected, so complex an apparatus was liable, like the Ptolemaic system of the heavens, to occasional derangements; however, by good luck, I was able to apply an easy remedy to these disorders which sometimes threatened to disturb the comfort, and even the serenity, of the great man.

Precisely at five minutes before five o'clock, winter or summer, Lampe, Kant's servant, who had formerly served in the army, marched into his master's room with the air of a sentinel on duty, and cried aloud in a military tone,—'Mr. Professor, the time is come.' This summons Kant invariably obeyed without one moment's delay, as a soldier does the word of command—never, under any circumstances, allowing himself a respite, not even under the rare accident of having passed a sleepless night. As the clock struck five, Kant was seated at the breakfast-table, where he drank what he called *one* cup of tea; and no doubt he thought it such; but the fact was, that in part from his habit of reverie, and in part also for the purpose of refreshing its warmth, he filled up his cup so often, that in general he is supposed to have drunk two, three, or some unknown number. Immediately after he smoked a pipe of tobacco, (the only one which he allowed himself through the entire day,) but so rapidly, that a pile of glowing embers remained unsmoked. During this operation he thought over his arrangements for the day, as he had done the evening before during the twilight. About seven he usually went to his lecture-room, and from that he returned to his writing-table. Precisely at three quarters before one he rose from his chair, and called aloud to the cook,—'It has struck three quarters.' The meaning of which summons was this:— Immediately after taking soup, it was his constant practice to swallow what he called a dram, which consisted either of Hungarian wine, of Rhenish, of a cordial, or (in default of these) of Bishop. A flask of this was brought up by the cook on the proclamation of the three quarters. Kant hurried with it to the eating-room, poured out his *quantum*, left it standing in readiness, covered, however, with paper, to prevent its becoming vapid, and then went back to his study, and awaited the arrival of his guests, whom to the latest period of his life he never received but in full dress.

Thus we come round again to dinner, and the reader has now an accurate picture of the course of Kant's day; the rigid monotony of which was not burthensome to him; and probably contributed, with the uniformity of his diet, and other habits of the same regularity, to lengthen his life. On this consideration, indeed, he had come to regard his health and his old age as in a great measure the product of his own exertions. He spoke of himself often under the figure of a gymnastic artist, who had continued for nearly fourscore years to support his balance upon the slack-rope of life, without once swerving to the right or to the left. In spite of every illness to which his constitutional tendencies had exposed him, he still kept his position in life triumphantly. However, he would sometimes observe sportively, that it was really absurd, and a sort of insult to the next generation for a man to live so long, because he thus interfered with the prospects of younger people.

This anxious attention to his health accounts for the great interest which he attached to all new discoveries in medicine, or to new ways of theorizing on the old ones. As a work of great pretension in both classes, he set the highest value upon the theory of the Scotch physician Brown, or (as it is usually called, from the Latin name of its author,) the Brunonian Theory. No sooner had Weikard adopted [7] and made it known in Germany, than Kant became familiar with it. He considered it not only as a great step taken for medicine, but even for the general interests of man, and fancied that in this he saw something analogous to the course which human nature has held in still more important inquiries, viz.: first of all, a continual ascent towards the more and more elaborately complex, and then a treading back, on its own steps, towards the simple and elementary. Dr. Beddoes's Essays, also, for producing by art and curing pulmonary consumption, and the method of Reich for curing fevers, made a powerful impression upon him; which, however, declined as those novelties (especially the last) began to sink in credit. As to Dr. Jenner's discovery of vaccination, he was less favorably disposed to it; he apprehended dangerous consequences from the absorption of a brutal miasma into the human blood, or at least into the lymph; and at any rate he thought, that, as a guarantee against the variolous infection, it required a much longer probation. Groundless as all these views were, it was exceedingly entertaining to hear the fertility of argument and analogy which he brought forward to support them. One of the subjects which occupied him at the latter end of his life, was the theory and phenomena of galvanism, which, however, he never satisfactorily mastered. Augustin's book upon this subject was about the last that he read, and his copy still retains on the margin his, pencil-marks of doubts, queries and suggestions.

The infirmities of age now began to steal upon Kant, and betrayed themselves in more shapes than one. Connected with Kant's prodigious memory for all things that had any intellectual bearings, he had from youth labored under an unusual weakness of this faculty in relation to the common affairs of daily life. Some remarkable instances of this are on record, from the period of his childish days; and now, when his second childhood was commencing, this infirmity increased upon him very sensibly. One of the first signs was, that he began to repeat the same stories more than once on the same day. Indeed, the decay of his memory was too palpable to escape his own notice; and, to provide against it, and secure himself from all apprehension of inflicting tedium upon his guests, he began to write a syllabus, or list of themes, for each day's conversation, on cards, or the covers of letters, or any chance scrap of paper. But these memoranda accumulated so fast upon him, and were so easily lost, or not forthcoming at the proper moment, that I prevailed on him to substitute a blank-paper book, which I had directed to be made, and which still remains, with some affecting memorials of his own conscious weakness. As often happens, however, in such cases, he had a perfect memory for the remote events of his life, and could repeat with great readiness, and without once stumbling, very long passages from German or Latin poems, especially from the AEneid, whilst the very words that had been uttered but a moment before dropped away from his remembrance. The past came forward with the distinctness and liveliness of an immediate existence, whilst the present faded away into the obscurity of infinite distance.

Another sign of his mental decay was the

weakness with which he now began to theo-
rize. He accounted for everything by electricity. A singular mortality at this time prevailed
amongst the cats of Vienna, Basle, Copen-
hagen, and other places. Cats being so emi-
nently an electric animal, of course he
attributed this epizootic to electricity. During
the same period, he persuaded himself that a
peculiar configuration of clouds prevailed; this
he took as a collateral proof of his electrical hy-
pothesis. His own headaches, too, which in all
probability were a mere remote effect of old
age, and a direct one of an inability [8] to think
as easily and as severely as formerly, he explained upon the same principle. And this was
a notion of which his friends were not anxious
to disabuse him, because, as something of the
same character of weather (and therefore probably the same general tendency of the electric
power) is found to prevail for whole cycles of
years, entrance upon another cycle held out to
him some prospect of relief. A delusion which
secured the comforts of hope was the next best
thing to an actual remedy; and a man who, in
such circumstances, is cured of his delusion,
*'cui demptus per vim mentis gratissimus error,'*

might reasonably have exclaimed, '*Pol, me oc-
cidistis, amici.*'

Possibly the reader may suppose, that, in
this particular instance of charging his own de-
cays upon the state of the atmosphere, Kant
was actuated by the weakness of vanity, or
some unwillingness to face the real fact that his
powers were decaying. But this was not the
case. He was perfectly aware of his own condition, and, as early as 1799, he said, in my presence, to a party of his friends—'Gentlemen, I
am old, and weak, and childish, and you must
treat me as a child.' Or perhaps it may be
thought that he shrank from the contemplation
of death, which, as apoplexy seemed to be
threatened by the pains in his head, might
have happened any day. But neither was this
the case. He now lived in a continual state of
resignation, and prepared to meet any dispen-
sation of Providence. 'Gentlemen,' said he one
day to his guests, 'I do not fear to die. I assure
you, as in the presence of God, that if I were
this night to be made suddenly aware that I
was on the point of being summoned, I would
raise my hands to heaven, fold them, and say,
Blessed be God! If indeed it were possible that

a whisper such as this could reach my ear—
Fourscore years thou hast lived, in which time
thou hast inflicted much evil upon thy fellow-
men, the case would be otherwise.' Whosoever
has heard Kant speak of his own death, will
bear witness to the tone of earnest sincerity
which, on such occasions, marked his manner
and utterance.

A third sign of his decaying faculties was,
that he now lost all accurate measure of time.
One minute, nay, without exaggeration, a
much less space of time, stretched out in his
apprehension of things to a wearisome duration. Of this I can give one rather amusing instance, which was of constant recurrence. At
the beginning of the last year of his life, he
fell into a custom of taking immediately after
dinner a cup of coffee, especially on those
days when it happened that I was of his
party. And such was the importance he attached to this little pleasure, that he would
even make a memorandum beforehand, in the
blank-paper book I had given him, that on the
next day I was to dine with him, and consequently that there was to be coffee. Sometimes it would happen, that the interest of

conversation carried him past the time at which he felt the craving for it; and this I was not sorry to observe, as I feared that coffee, which he had never been accustomed to, [9] might disturb his rest at night. But, if this did not happen, then commenced a scene of some interest. Coffee must be brought 'upon the spot,' (a word he had constantly in his mouth during his latter days,) 'in a moment.' And the expressions of his impatience, though from old habit still gentle, were so lively, and had so much of infantine naïveté about them, that none of us could forbear smiling. Knowing what would happen, I had taken care that all the preparations should be made beforehand; the coffee was ground; the water was boiling; and the very moment the word was given, his servant shot in like an arrow, and plunged the coffee into the water. All that remained, therefore, was to give it time to boil up. But this trifling delay seemed unendurable to Kant. All consolations were thrown away upon him: vary the formula as we might, he was never at a loss for a reply. If it was said—'Dear Professor, the coffee will be brought up in a moment.'—'*Will* be!' he would say, 'but there's the rub, that it only *will* be:

Man never *is*, but always *to be* blest.'

If another cried out—'The coffee is coming immediately.'—'Yes,' he would retort, 'and so is the next hour: and, by the way, it's about that length of time that I have waited for it.' Then he would collect himself with a stoical air, and say—'Well, one can die after all: it is but dying; and in the next world, thank God! there is no drinking of coffee, and consequently no—waiting for it.' Sometimes he would rise from his chair, open the door, and cry out with a feeble querulousness—'Coffee! coffee!' And when at length he heard the servant's step upon the stairs, he would turn round to us, and, as joyfully as ever sailor from the mast-head, he would call out—'Land, land! my dear friends, I see land.'

This general decline in Kant's powers, active and passive, gradually brought about a revolution in his habits of life. Heretofore, as I have already mentioned, he went to bed at ten, and rose a little before five. The latter practice

he still observed, but not the other. In 1802 he
retired as early as nine, and afterwards still
earlier. He found himself so much refreshed by
this addition to his rest, that at first he was disposed to utter a *Euraeka*, as over some great
discovery in the art of restoring exhausted nature: but afterwards, on pushing it still farther,
he did not find the success answer his expecta-
tions. His walks he now limited to a few turns
in the King's gardens, which were at no great
distance from his own house. In order to walk
more firmly, he adopted a peculiar method of
stepping; he carried his foot to the ground, not
forward, and obliquely, but perpendicularly,
and with a kind of stamp, so as to secure a
larger basis, by setting down the entire sole at
once. Notwithstanding this precaution, upon
one occasion he fell in the street. He was quite
unable to raise himself; and two young ladies,
who saw the accident, ran to his assistance.
With his usual graciousness of manner he
thanked them fervently for their assistance,
and presented one of them with a rose which
he happened to have in his hand. This lady
was not personally known to Kant; but she
was greatly delighted with his little present,

and still keeps the rose as a frail memorial of her transitory interview with the great philosopher.

This accident, as I have reason to think, was the cause of his henceforth renouncing exercise altogether. All labors, even that of reading, were now performed slowly, and with manifest effort; and those which cost him any bodily exertion became very exhausting to him. His feet refused to do their office more and more; he fell continually, both when moving across the room, and even when standing still: yet he seldom suffered from these falls; and he constantly laughed at them, maintaining that it was impossible he could hurt himself, from the extreme lightness of his person, which was indeed by this time the merest skeleton. Very often, especially in the morning, he dropped asleep in his chair from pure weariness: on these occasions he fell forward upon the floor, and lay there unable to raise himself up, until accident brought one of his servants or his friends into the room. Afterwards these falls were prevented, by substituting a chair with circular supports, that met and clasped in front.

These unseasonable dozings exposed him to another danger. He fell repeatedly, whilst reading, with his head into the candles; a cotton night-cap which he wore was instantly in a blaze, and flaming about his head. Whenever this happened, Kant behaved with great presence of mind. Disregarding the pain, he seized the blazing cap, drew it from his head, laid it quietly on the floor, and trod out the flames with his feet. Yet, as this last act brought his dressing-gown into a dangerous neighborhood to the flames, I changed the form of his cap, persuaded him to arrange the candles differently, and had a decanter of water placed constantly by his side; and in this way I applied a remedy to a danger, which would else probably have been fatal to him.

From the sallies of impatience, which I have described in the case of the coffee, there was reason to fear that, with the increasing infirmities of Kant, would grow up a general waywardness and obstinacy of temper. For my own sake, therefore, and not less for his, I now laid down one rule for my future conduct in his house; which was, that I would, on no occasion, allow my reverence for him to interfere with the firmest expression of my opinion on subjects relating to his own health; and in cases of great importance, that I would make no compromise with his particular humors, but insist, not only on my view of the case, but also on the practical adoption of my views; or, if this were refused me, that I would take my departure at once, and not be made responsible for the comfort of a person whom I had no power to influence. And this behavior on my part it was that won Kant's confidence; for there was nothing which disgusted him so much as any approach to fawning or sycophancy. As his imbecility increased, he became daily more liable to mental delusions; and, in particular, he fell into many fantastic notions about the conduct of his servants, and, in consequence, into a peevish mode of treating them. Upon these occasions I generally observed a deep silence. But sometimes he would ask me for my opinion; and when this happened, I did not scruple to say, 'Ingenuously, then, Mr. Professor, I think that you are in the wrong.'—'You think so?' he would reply calmly, at the same time asking for my reasons, which he would listen to with great patience, and openness to conviction. Indeed, it was evident that the firmest opposition, so long as it rested upon assignable grounds and principles, won upon his regard; whilst his own nobleness of character still moved him to habitual contempt for timorous and partial acquiescence in his opinions, even when his infirmities made him most anxious for such acquiescence.

Earlier in life Kant had been little used to contradiction. His superb understanding, his brilliancy in conversation, founded in part upon his ready and sometimes rather caustic wit, and in part upon his prodigious command of knowledge—the air of noble self-confidence which the consciousness of these advantages impressed upon his manners—and the general knowledge of the severe innocence of his life—all combined to give him a station of superiority to others, which generally secured him from open contradiction. And if it sometimes happened that he met a noisy and intemperate opposition, supported by any pretences to wit, he usually withdrew himself from that sort of unprofitable altercation with dignity, by contriving to give such a turn to the conversation as won the general favor of the company to himself, and impressed, silence, or modesty at least, upon the boldest disputant. From a person so little familiar with opposition, it could scarcely have been anticipated that he should daily surrender his wishes to mine—if not without discussion, yet always without displeasure. So, however, it was. No habit, of whatever long standing, could be objected to as injurious to his health, but he would generally renounce it. And he had this excellent custom in such cases, that either he would resolutely and at once decide for his own opinion, or, if he professed to follow his friend's, he would follow it sincerely, and not try it unfairly by trying it imperfectly. Any plan, however trifling, which he had once consented to adopt on the suggestion of another, was never afterwards defeated or embarrassed by unseasonable interposition from his own humors. And thus, the very period of his decay drew forth so many fresh expressions of his character, in its amiable or noble features, as daily increased my affection and reverence for his person.

Having mentioned his servants, I shall here

take occasion to give some account of his man-servant Lampe. It was a great misfortune for Kant, in his old age and infirmities, that this man also became old, and subject to a different sort of infirmities. This Lampe had originally served in the Prussian army; on quitting which he entered the service of Kant. In this situation he had lived about forty years; and, though always dull and stupid, had, in the early part of this period, discharged his duties with tolerable fidelity. But latterly, presuming upon his own indispensableness, from his perfect knowledge of all the domestic arrangements, and upon his master's weakness, he had fallen into great irregularities and neglect of his duties. Kant had been obliged, therefore, of late, to threaten repeatedly that he would discharge him. I, who knew that Kant, though one of the kindest-hearted men, was also one of the firmest, foresaw that this discharge, once given, would be irrevocable: for the word of Kant was as sacred as other men's oaths. Consequently, upon every opportunity, I remonstrated with Lampe on the folly of his conduct, and his wife joined me on these occasions. Indeed, it was high time that a change should be made in some quarter; for it now became dangerous to leave Kant, who was constantly falling from weakness, to the care of an old ruffian, who was himself apt to fall from intoxication. The fact was, that from the moment I undertook the management of Kant's affairs, Lampe saw there was an end to his old system of abusing his master's confidence in pecuniary affairs, and the other advantages which he took of his helpless situation. This made him desperate, and he behaved worse and worse; until one morning, in January, 1802, Kant told me, that, humiliating as he felt such a confession, the fact was, that Lampe had just treated him in a way which he was ashamed to repeat. I was too much shocked to distress him by inquiring into the particulars. But the result was, that Kant now insisted, temperately but firmly, on Lampe's dismissal. Accordingly, a new servant, of the name of Kaufmann, was immediately engaged; and on the next day Lampe was discharged with a handsome pension for life.

Here I must mention a little circumstance which does honor to Kant's benevolence. In his last will, on the assumption that Lampe would continue with him to his death, he had made a very liberal provision for him; but upon this new arrangement of the pension, which was to take effect immediately, it became necessary to revoke that part of his will, which he did in a separate codicil, that began thus:—'In consequence of the ill behavior of my servant Lampe, I think fit,' &c. But soon after, considering that such a record of Lampe's misconduct might be seriously injurious to his interests, he cancelled the passage, and expressed it in such a way, that no trace remained behind of his just displeasure. And his benign nature was gratified with knowing, that, this one sentence blotted out, there remained no other in all his numerous writings, published or confidential, which spoke the language of anger, or could leave any ground for doubting that he died in charity with all the world. Upon Lampe's calling to demand a written character, he was, however, a good deal embarrassed; his stern reverence for truth being, in this instance, armed against the first impulses of his kindness. Long and anxiously he sat, with the certificate lying before him, debating how he should fill up the blanks. I was present, but in such a matter I did not take the liberty of suggesting any advice. At last, he took his pen, and filled up the blank as follows:—'—has served me long and faithfully,'—(for Kant was not aware that he had robbed him,)—'but did not display those particular qualifications which fitted him for waiting on an old and infirm man like myself.'

This scene of disturbance over, which to Kant, a lover of peace and tranquillity, caused a shock that he would gladly have been spared; it was fortunate that no other of that nature occurred during the rest of his life. Kaufmann, the successor of Lampe, turned out to be a respectable and upright man, and soon conceived a great attachment to his master's person. Things now put on a new face in Kant's family: by the removal of one of the belligerents, peace was once more restored amongst his servants; for hitherto there had been eternal wars between Lampe and the cook. Sometimes it was Lampe that carried a war of aggression into the cook's territory of the kitchen; sometimes it was the cook that revenged these insults, by sallying out upon Lampe in the neutral ground of the hall, or invaded him even in his own sanctuary of the butler's pantry. The uproars were everlasting; and thus far it was fortunate for the peace of the philosopher, that his hearing had begun to fail; by which means he was spared many an exhibition of hateful passions and ruffian violence, which annoyed his guests and friends. But now all things had changed: deep silence reigned in the pantry; the kitchen rang no more with martial alarums; and the hall was unvexed with skirmish or pursuit. Yet it may be readily supposed that to Kant, at the age of seventy-eight, changes, even for the better, were not welcome: so intense had been the uniformity of his life and habits, that the least innovation in the arrangement of articles as trifling as a penknife, or a pair of scissors, disturbed him; and not merely if they were pushed two or three inches out of their customary position, but even if they were laid a little awry; and as to larger objects, such as chairs, &c., any dislocation of their usual arrangement, any trans position, or addition to their number, perfectly confounded him; and his eye appeared restlessly to haunt the seat of the mal-arrangement, until the ancient order was restored. With such habits the reader may conceive how distressing it must have been to him, at this period of decaying powers, to adapt himself to a new servant, a new voice, a new step, &c.

Aware of this, I had on the day before he entered upon his duties, written down for the new servant upon a sheet of paper the entire routine of Kant's daily life, down to the minutest and most trivial circumstances; all which he mastered with the greatest rapidity. To make sure, however, we went through a rehearsal of the whole ritual; he performing the manoeuvres, I looking on and giving the word. Still I felt uneasy at the idea of his being left entirely to his own discretion on his first *debut* in good earnest, and therefore I made a point of attending on this important day; and in the few instances where the new recruit missed the accurate manoeuvre, a glance or a nod from me easily made him comprehend his failure.

One part only there was of the daily ceremonial, where all of us were at a loss, as it was a part which no mortal eyes had ever witnessed but those of Lampe: this was breakfast. However, that we might do all in our power, I myself attended at four o'clock in the morning. The day happened, as I remember, to be the 1st of February, 1802. Precisely at five, Kant made his appearance; and nothing could equal his astonishment on finding me in the room. Fresh from the confusion of dreaming, and bewildered alike by the sight of his new servant, by Lampe's absence, and by my presence, he could with difficulty be made to comprehend the purpose of my visit. A friend in need is a friend indeed; and we would now have given any money to that learned person who could have instructed us in the arrangement of the breakfast table. But this was a mystery revealed to none but Lampe. At length Kant took this task upon himself; and apparently all was now settled to his satisfaction. Yet still it struck me that he was under some embarrassment or constraint. Upon this I said—that, with his permission, I would take a cup of tea, and afterwards smoke a pipe with him. He accepted my offer with his usual courteous demeanor; but seemed unable to familiarize himself with the novelty of his situation. I was at this time sitting directly opposite to him; and at last he frankly told me, but with the kindest and most apologetic air, that he was really under the necessity of begging that I would sit out of his sight; for that, having sat alone at the breakfast table for considerably more than half a century, he could not abruptly adapt his mind to a change in this respect; and he found his thoughts very sensibly disturbed. I did as he desired; the servant retired into an antiroom, where he waited within call; and Kant recovered his wonted composure. Just the same scene passed over again, when I called at the same hour on a fine summer morning some months after.

Henceforth all went right: or, if occasionally some little mistake occurred, Kant showed himself very considerate and indulgent, and would remark of his own accord, that a new servant could not be expected to know all his peculiar ways and humors. In one respect, indeed, this man adapted himself to Kant's scholarlike taste, in a way which Lampe was incapable of doing. Kant was somewhat fastidious in matters of pronunciation; and this man had a great facility in catching the true sound of Latin words, the titles of books, and the names or designations of Kant's friends: not one of which accomplishments could Lampe, the most insufferable of blockheads, ever attain to. In particular, I have been told by Kant's old friends, that for the space of more than thirty years, during which he had been in the habit of reading the newspaper published by Hartung, Lampe delivered it with the same identical blunder on every day of publication.—'Mr. Professor, here is Hart*mann's* journal.' Upon which Kant would reply—'Eh! what?—What's that you say? Hartmann's journal? I tell you, it is not Hartmann, but Hartung: now, repeat it after me—not Hartmann, but Hartung.' Then Lampe, looking sulky, and drawing himself up with the stiff air of a soldier on guard, and in the very same monotonous tone with which he had been used to sing out his challenge of —*Who goes there?* would roar—'not Hartmann, but Hartung.' 'Now again!' Kant would say: on which again Lampe roared—'not Hartmann, but Hartung.' 'Now a third time,' cried Kant: on which for a third time the unhappy Lampe would howl out—'not Hartmann, but Hartung.' And this whimsical scene of parade duty was continually repeated: duly as the day of publication came, the irreclaimable old dunce was put through the same manoeuvres, which were as invariably followed by the same blunder on the next. In spite, however, of this advantage, in the new servant, and his general superiority to his predecessor, Kant's nature was too kind and good, and too indulgent to all people's infirmities but his own, not to miss the voice and the 'old familiar face' that he had been accustomed to for forty years. And I met with what struck me as an affecting instance of Kant's yearning after his old good-for-nothing servant in his memorandum-book: other people record what they wish to remember; but Kant had here recorded what he was to forget. 'Mem.: February, 1802, the name of Lampe must now be remembered no more.'

In the spring of this year, 1802, I advised Kant to take the air. It was very long since he had been out of doors, [10] and walking was now out of the question. But I thought the motion of a carriage and the air would be likely to revive him. On the power of vernal sights and sounds I did not much rely; for these had long ceased to affect him. Of all the changes that spring brings with it, there was one only that now interested Kant; and he longed for it with an eagerness and intensity of expectation, that it was almost painful to witness: this was the return of a hedge sparrow that sang in his garden, and before his window. This bird, either the same, or one of the next generation, had sung for years in the same situation; and Kant grew uneasy when the cold weather, lasting longer than usual, retarded its return. Like Lord Bacon, indeed, he had a childlike love for birds in general, and in particular, took pains to encourage the sparrows to build above the windows of his study; and when this happened, (as it often did, from the silence which prevailed in his study,) he watched their proceedings with the delight and the tenderness which others give to a human interest. To return to the point I was speaking of, Kant was at first very unwilling to accede to my proposal of going abroad. 'I shall sink down in the carriage,' said he, 'and fall together like a heap of old rags.' But I persisted with a gentle importunity in urging him to the attempt, assuring him that we would return immediately if he found the effort too much for him. Accordingly, upon a tolerably warm day of early [11] summer, I, and an old friend of Kant's, accompanied him to a little place which I rented in the country. As we drove through the streets, Kant was delighted to find that he could sit upright, and bear the motion of the carriage, and seemed to draw youthful pleasure from the sight of the towers and other public buildings, which he had not seen for years. We reached the place of our destination in high spirits. Kant drank a cup of coffee, and attempted to smoke a little. After this, he sat and sunned himself, listening with delight to the warbling of birds, which congregated in great numbers about this spot. He distinguished every bird by its song, and called it by its right name. After staying about half an hour, we set off on our homeward journey, Kant still cheerful, but apparently satiated with his day's enjoyment.

I had on this occasion purposely avoided taking him to any public gardens, that I might not disturb his pleasure by exposing him to the distressing gaze of public curiosity. However, it was known in Königsberg that Kant had gone out; and accordingly, as the carriage moved through the streets which led to his residence, there was a general rush from all quarters in that direction, and, when we turned into the street where the house stood, we found it already choked up with people. As we slowly drew up to the door, a lane was formed in the crowd, through which Kant was led, I and my friend supporting him on our arms. Looking at the crowd, I observed the faces of many persons of rank, and distinguished strangers, some of whom now saw Kant for the first time, and many of them for the last.

As the winter of 1802-3 approached, he complained more than ever of an affection of the stomach, which no medical man had been able to mitigate, or even to explain. The winter passed over in a complaining way; he was weary of life, and longed for the hour of dismission. 'I can be of service to the world no more,' said he, 'and am a burden to myself.' Often I endeavored to cheer him by the anticipation of excursions that we would make together when summer came again. On these he calculated with so much earnestness, that he had made a regular scale or classification of them—1. Airings; 2. Journeys; 3. Travels. And nothing could equal the yearning impatience expressed for the coming of spring and summer, not so much for their own peculiar attractions, as because they were the seasons for travelling. In his memorandum-book, he made this note:—'The three summer months are June, July, and August'— meaning that they were the three months for travelling. And in conversation he expressed the feverish strength of his wishes so plaintively and affectingly, that everybody was drawn into powerful sympathy with him, and wished for some magical means of ante-dating the course of the seasons.

In this winter his bed-room was often warmed. This was the room in which he kept his little collection of books, of about four hundred and fifty volumes, chiefly presentation-copies from the authors. It may seem singular that Kant, who read so extensively, should have no larger library; but he had less need of one than most scholars, having in his earlier years been librarian at the Royal Library of the Castle; and since then having enjoyed from the liberality of Hartknoch, his publisher, (who, in his turn, had profited by the liberal terms on which Kant had made over to him the copyright of his own works,) the first sight of every new book that appeared.

At the close of this winter, that is in 1803, Kant first began to complain of unpleasant dreams, sometimes of very terrific ones, which awakened him in great agitation. Oftentimes melodies, which he had heard in earliest youth sung in the streets of Königsberg, resounded painfully in his ears, and dwelt upon them in a way from which no efforts of abstraction could release him. These kept him awake to unseasonable hours; and often when, after long watching, he had fallen asleep, however deep his sleep might be, it was suddenly broken up by terrific dreams, which alarmed him beyond description. Almost every night, the bell-rope, which communicated with a bell in the room above his own, where his servant slept, was pulled violently, and with the utmost agitation. No matter how fast the servant might hurry down, he was almost always too late, and was pretty sure to find his master out of bed, and often making his way in terror to some other part of the house. The weakness of his feet exposed him to such dreadful falls on these occasions, that at length (but with much difficulty)

I persuaded him to let his servant sleep in the same room with himself.

The morbid affection of the stomach began now to be more and more distressing; and he tried various applications, which he had formerly been loud in condemning, such as a few drops of rum upon a piece of sugar, naphtha, [12] &c. But all these were only palliatives; for his advanced age precluded the hope of a radical cure. His dreadful dreams became continually more appalling: single scenes, or passages in these dreams, were sufficient to compose the whole course of mighty tragedies, the impression from which was so profound as to stretch far into his waking hours. Amongst other phantasmata more shocking and indescribable, his dreams constantly represented to him the forms of murderers advancing to his bedside; and so agitated was he by the awful trains of phantoms that swept past him nightly, that in the first confusion of awaking he generally mistook his servant, who was hastening to his assistance, for a murderer. In the day-time we often conversed upon these shadowy illusions; and Kant, with his usual spirit of stoical contempt for nervous weakness of every sort, laughed at them; and, to fortify his own resolution to contend against them, he wrote down in his memorandum-book, 'There must be no yielding to panics of darkness.' At my suggestion, however, he now burned a light in his chamber, so placed as that the rays might be shaded from his face. At first he was very averse to this, though gradually he became reconciled to it. But that he could bear it at all, was to me an expression of the great revolution accomplished by the terrific agency of his dreams. Heretofore, darkness and utter silence were the two pillars on which his sleep rested: no step must approach his room; and as to light, if he saw but a moonbeam penetrating a crevice of the shutters, it made him unhappy; and, in fact, the windows of his bed-chamber were barricaded night and day. But now darkness was a terror to him, and silence an oppression. In addition to his lamp, therefore, he had now a repeater in his room; the sound was at first too loud, but, after muffling the hammer with cloth, both the ticking and the striking became companionable sounds to him.

At this time (spring of 1803) his appetite began to fail, which I thought no good sign.

Many persons insist that Kant was in the habit of eating too much for health. [13] I, however, cannot assent to this opinion; for he ate but once a day, and drank no beer. Of this liquor, (I mean the strong black beer,) he was, indeed, the most determined enemy. If ever a man died prematurely, Kant would say—'He has been drinking beer, I presume.' Or, if another were indisposed, you might be sure he would ask, 'But does he drink beer?' And, according to the answer on this point, he regulated his anticipations for the patient. Strong beer, in short, he uniformly maintained to be a slow poison. Voltaire, by the way, had said to a young physician who denounced coffee under the same bad name of a 'slow poison,' 'You're right there, my friend, however; slow it is, and horribly slow; for I have been drinking it these seventy years, and it has not killed me yet;' but this was an answer which, in the case of beer, Kant would not allow of.

On the 22d of April, 1803, his birth-day, the last which he lived to see, was celebrated in a full assembly of his friends. This festival he had long looked forward to with great expectation, and delighted even to hear the progress made in the preparations for it. But when the day came, the over- excitement and tension of expectation seemed to have defeated itself. He tried to appear happy; but the bustle of a numerous company confounded and distressed him; and his spirits were manifestly forced. He seemed first to revive to any real sense of pleasure at night, when the company had departed, and he was undressing in his study. He then talked with much pleasure about the presents which, as usual, would be made to his servants on this occasion; for Kant was never happy himself, unless he saw all around him happy. He was a great maker of presents; but at the same time he had no toleration for the studied theatrical effect, the accompaniment of formal congratulations, and the sentimental pathos with which birth-day presents are made in Germany. [14] In all this, his masculine taste gave him a sense of something fade and ludicrous.

The summer of 1803 was now come, and, visiting Kant one day, I was thunderstruck to hear him direct me, in the most serious tone, to provide the funds necessary for an extensive foreign tour. I made no opposition, but asked his reasons for such a plan; he alleged the miserable sensations he had in his stomach, which were no longer endurable. Knowing what power over Kant a quotation from a Roman poet had always had, I simply replied—'Post equitem sedet atra cura,' and for the present he said no more. But the touching and pathetic earnestness with which he was continually ejaculating prayers for warmer weather, made it doubtful to me whether his wishes on this point ought not, partially at least, to be gratified; and I therefore proposed to him a little excursion to the cottage we had visited the year before. 'Anywhere,' said he, 'no matter whither, provided it be far enough.' Towards the latter end of June, therefore, we executed this scheme; on getting into the carriage, the order of the day with Kant was, 'Distance, distance. Only let us go far enough,' said he: but scarcely had we reached the city-gates before the journey seemed already to have lasted too long. On reaching the cottage we found coffee waiting for us; but he would scarcely allow himself time for drinking it, before he ordered the carriage to the door; and the journey back seemed insupportably long to him, though it was performed in something less than twenty minutes. 'Is this never to have an end?' was his continual exclamation; and great was his joy when he found himself once more in his study, undressed, and in bed. And for this night he slept in peace, and once again was liberated from the persecution of dreams.

Soon after he began again to talk of journeys, of travels in remote countries, &c., and, in consequence, we repeated our former excursion several times; and though the circumstances were pretty nearly the same on every occasion, and always terminating in disappointment as to the immediate pleasure anticipated, yet, undoubtedly, they were, on the whole, salutary to his spirits. In particular, the cottage itself, standing under the shelter of tall alders, with a valley stretched beneath it, through which a little brook meandered, broken by a water-fall, whose pealing sound dwelt pleasantly on the ear, sometimes, on a quiet sunny day, gave a lively delight to Kant: and once, under accidental circumstances of summer clouds and sun-lights, the little pastoral landscape suddenly awakened a lively remembrance which had been long laid asleep, of a heavenly summer morning in youth, which he had passed in a bower upon the banks of a rivulet that ran through the grounds of a dear and early friend, Gen. Von Lossow. The strength of the impression was such, that he seemed actually to be living over that morning again, thinking as he then thought, and conversing with those that were no more.

His very last excursion was in August of this year, (1803,) not to my cottage, but to the garden of a friend. But on this day he manifested great impatience. It had been arranged that he was to meet an old friend at the gardens; and I, with two other gentlemen, attended him. It happened that *out* party arrived first; and such was Kant's weakness, and total loss of power to estimate the duration of time, that, after waiting a few moments, he insisted that some hours had elapsed—that his friend could not be expected—and went away in great discomposure of mind. And so ended Kant's travelling in this world.

In the beginning of autumn the sight of his right eye began to fail him; the left he had long lost the use of. This earliest of his losses, by the way, he discovered by mere accident, and without any previous warning. Sitting down one day to rest himself in the course of a walk, it occurred to him that he would try the comparative strength of his eyes; but on taking out a newspaper which he had in his pocket, he was surprised to find that with his left eye he could not distinguish a letter. In earlier life he had two remarkable affections of the eyes: once, on returning from a walk, he saw objects double for a long space of time; and twice he became stone-blind. Whether these accidents are to be considered as uncommon, I leave to the decision of oculists. Certain it is, they gave very little disturbance to Kant; who, until old age had reduced his powers, lived in a constant state of stoical preparation for the worst that could befall him. I was now shocked to think of the degree in which his burthensome sense of dependence would be aggravated, if he should totally lose the power of sight. As it was, he read and wrote with great difficulty: in fact, his writing was little better than that which most people can produce as a trial of skill with their eyes shut. From old habits of solitary study, he had no pleasure in hearing others read to him; and he daily distressed me by the pathetic earnestness of his entreaties that I would have a reading-glass devised for him. Whatever my own optical skill could suggest, I tried; and the best opticians were sent for to bring their glasses, and take his directions for altering them; but all was to no purpose.

In this last year of his life Kant very unwillingly received the visits of strangers; and, unless under particular circumstances, wholly declined them. Yet, when travellers had come a very great way out of their road to see him, I confess that I was at a loss how to conduct myself. To have refused too pertinaciously, could not but give me the air of wishing to make myself of importance. And I must acknowledge, that, amongst some instances of importunity and coarse expressions of low-bred curiosity, I witnessed, on the part of many people of rank, a most delicate sensibility to the condition of the aged recluse. On sending in their cards, they would generally accompany them by some message, expressive of their unwillingness to gratify their wish to see him at any risk of distressing him. The fact was, that such visits *did* distress him much; for he felt it a

degradation to be exhibited in his helpless
state, when he was aware of his own inca-
pacity to meet properly the attention that was
paid to him. Some, however, were admitted, [15]
according to the circumstances of the case, and
the state of Kant's spirits at the moment.
Amongst these, I remember that we were par-
ticularly pleased with M. Otto, the same who
signed the treaty of peace between France and
England with the present Lord Liverpool,
(then Lord Hawkesbury.) A young Russian
also rises to my recollection at this moment,
from the excessive (and I think unaffected) enthusiasm which he displayed. On being introduced to Kant, he advanced hastily, took both
his hands, and kissed them. Kant, who, from
living so much amongst his English friends,
had a good deal of the English dignified reserve about him, and hated anything like
*scenes*, appeared to shrink a little from this
mode of salutation, and was rather embarrassed. However, the young man's manner, I
believe, was not at all beyond his genuine feel-
ings; for next day he called again, made some
inquiries about Kant's health, was very anxious to know whether his old age were bur-

thensome to him, and above all things entreated for some little memorial of the great man to carry away with him. By accident the servant had found a small cancelled fragment of the original MS. of Kant's 'Anthropologie:' this, with my sanction, he gave to the Russian; who received it with rapture, kissed it, and then gave him in return the only dollar he had about him; and, thinking that not enough, actually pulled off his coat and waistcoat and forced them upon the man. Kant, whose native simplicity of character very much indisposed him to sympathy with any extravagances of feeling, could not, however, forbear smiling good- humoredly on being made acquainted with this instance of *naïveté* and enthusiasm in his young admirer.

I now come to an event in Kant's life, which ushered in its closing stage. On the 8th of October, 1803, for the first time since his youth, he was seriously ill. When a student at the University, he had once suffered from an ague, which, however, gave way to pedestrian exercise; and in later years, he had endured some pain from a contusion on his head; but, with these two exceptions, (if they can be considered such,) he had never (properly speaking) been ill. The cause of his illness was this: his appetite had latterly been irregular, or rather I should say depraved; and he no longer took pleasure in anything but bread and butter, and English cheese. [16] On the 7th of October, at dinner, he ate little else, in spite of everything that I and another friend then dining with him, could urge to dissuade him. And for the first time I fancied that he seemed displeased with my importunity, as though I were overstepping the just line of my duties. He insisted that the cheese never had done him any harm, nor would now. I had no course left me but to hold my tongue; and he did as he pleased. The consequence was what might have been anticipated—a restless night, succeeded by a day of memorable illness. The next morning all went on as usual, till nine o'clock, when Kant, who was then leaning on his sister's arm, suddenly fell senseless to the ground. A messenger was immediately despatched for me; and I hurried down to his house, where I found him lying in his bed, which had now been removed into his study, speechless and insensible. I had already summoned his physician; but, before he arrived, nature put forth efforts which brought Kant a little to himself. In about an hour he opened his eyes, and continued to mutter unintelligibly till towards the evening, when he rallied a little, and began to talk rationally. For the first time in his life, he was now, for a few days, confined to his bed, and ate nothing. On the 12th October, he again took some refreshment, and would have had his favorite food; but I was now resolved, at any risk of his displeasure, to oppose him firmly. I therefore stated to him the whole consequences of his last indulgence, of all which he manifestly had no recollection. He listened to what I said very attentively, and calmly expressed his conviction that I was perfectly in the wrong; but for the present he submitted. However, some days after, I found that he had offered a florin for a little bread and cheese, and then a dollar, and even more. Being again refused, he complained heavily; but gradually he weaned himself from asking for it, though at times he betrayed involuntarily how much he desired it.

On the 13th of October, his usual dinner parties were resumed, and he was considered convalescent; but it was seldom indeed that he recovered the tone of tranquil spirits which he had preserved until his late attack. Hitherto he had always loved to prolong this meal, the only one he took—or, as he expressed it in classical phrase, 'coenam *ducere*;' but now it was difficult to hurry it over fast enough for his wishes. From dinner, which terminated about two o'clock, he went straight to bed, and at intervals fell into slumbers; from which, however, he was regularly awoke by phantasmata or terrific dreams. At seven in the evening came on duly a period of great agitation, which lasted till five or six in the morning—sometimes later; and he continued through the night alternately to walk about and lie down, occasionally tranquil, but more often in great distress. It now became necessary that somebody should sit up with him, his man-servant being wearied out with the toils of the day. No person seemed to be so proper for this office as his sister, both as having long received a very liberal pension from him, and also as his nearest relative, who would be the best witness to the fact that her illustrious brother had wanted no comforts or attention in his last hours, which his situation admitted of. Accordingly she was applied to, and undertook to watch him alternately with his footman—a separate table being kept for her, and a very handsome addition made to her allowance. She turned out to be a quiet gentle-minded woman, who raised no disturbances amongst the servants, and soon won her brother's regard by the modest and retiring style of her manners; I may add, also, by the truly sisterly affection which she displayed towards him to the last.

The 8th of October had grievously affected Kant's faculties, but had not wholly destroyed them. For short intervals the clouds seemed to roll away that had settled upon his majestic intellect, and it shone forth as heretofore. During these moments of brief self-possession, his wonted benignity returned to him; and he expressed his gratitude for the exertions of those about him, and his sense of the trouble they underwent, in a very affecting way. With regard to his man-servant in particular, he was very anxious that he should be rewarded by liberal presents; and he pressed me earnestly on no account to be parsimonious. Indeed Kant was nothing less than princely in his use of money; and there was no occasion on which he was known to express the passion of scorn very powerfully, but when he was commenting on mean and penurious acts or habits. Those who knew him only in the streets, fancied that he was not liberal; for he steadily refused, upon principle, to relieve all common beggars. But, on the other hand, he was liberal to the public charitable institutions; he secretly assisted his own poor relations in a much ampler way than could reasonably have been expected of him; and it now appeared that he had many other deserving pensioners upon his bounty; a fact that was utterly unknown to any of us, until his increasing blindness and other infirmities devolved the duty of paying these pensions upon myself. It must be recollected, also, that Kant's whole fortune, which amounted to about twenty thousand dollars, was the product of his own honorable toils for nearly threescore years; and that he had himself suffered all the hardships of poverty in his youth, though he never once ran into any man's debt,—circumstances in his history, which, as they express how fully he must have been acquainted with the value of

money, greatly enhance the merit of his mu-
nificence.

In December, 1803, he became incapable of
signing his name. His sight, indeed, had for
some time failed him so much, that at dinner
he could not find his spoon without assistance;
and, when I happened to dine with him, I first
cut in pieces whatever was on his plate, next
put it into a spoon, and then guided his hand
to find the spoon. But his inability to sign his
name did not arise merely from blindness: the
fact was, that, from irretention of memory, he
could not recollect the letters which composed
his name; and, when they were repeated to
him, he could not represent the figure of the
letters in his imagination. At the latter end of
November, I had remarked that these incapaci-
ties were rapidly growing upon him, and in
consequence I prevailed on him to sign beforehand all the receipts, &c., which would be
wanted at the end of the year; and, afterwards,
on my representation, to prevent all disputes,
he gave me a regular legal power to sign on his
behalf.

Much as Kant was now reduced, yet he had
occasionally moods of social hilarity. His birth-

day was always an agreeable subject to him: some weeks before his death, I was calculating the time which it still wanted of that anniversary, and cheering him with the prospect of the rejoicings which would then take place: 'All your old friends,' said I, 'will meet together, and drink a glass of champagne to your health.' 'That,' said he, 'must be done upon the spot:' and he was not satisfied till the party was actually assembled. He drank a glass of wine with them, and with great elevation of spirits celebrated this birth-day which he was destined never to see.

In the latter weeks of his life, however, a great change took place in the tone of his spirits. At his dinner-table, where heretofore such a cloudless spirit of joviality had reigned, there was now a melancholy silence. It disturbed him to see his two dinner companions conversing privately together, whilst he himself sat like a mute on the stage with no part to perform. Yet to have engaged him in the conversation would have been still more distressing; for his hearing was now very imperfect; the effort to hear was itself painful to him; and his expressions, even when his thoughts were accurate enough, became nearly unintelligible. It is remarkable, however, that at the very lowest point of his depression, when he became perfectly incapable of conversing with any rational meaning on the ordinary affairs of life, he was still able to answer correctly and distinctly, in a degree that was perfectly astonishing, upon any question of philosophy or of science, especially of physical geography, [17] chemistry, or natural history. He talked satisfactorily, in his very worst state, of the gases, and stated very accurately different propositions of Kepler's, especially the law of the planetary motions. And I remember in particular, that upon the very last Monday of his life, when the extremity of his weakness moved a circle of his friends to tears, and he sat amongst us insensible to all we could say to him, cowering down, or rather I might say collapsing into a shapeless heap upon his chair, deaf, blind, torpid, motionless,—even then I whispered to the others that I would engage that Kant should take his part in conversation with propriety and animation. This they found it difficult to believe. Upon which I drew close to his ear, and put a question to him about the

Moors of Barbary. To the surprise of everybody but myself, he immediately gave us a summary account of their habits and customs; and told us by the way, that in the word *Algiers*, the *g* ought to be pronounced hard (as in the English word *gear*).

During the last fortnight of Kant's life, he busied himself unceasingly in a way that seemed not merely purposeless but self-contradictory. Twenty times in a minute he would unloose and tie his neck handkerchief—so also with a sort of belt which he wore about his dressing-gown, the moment it was clasped, he unclasped it with impatience, and was then equally impatient to have it clasped again. But no description can convey an adequate impression of the weary restlessness with which from morning to night he pursued these labors of Sisyphus—doing and undoing—fretting that he could not do it, fretting that he had done it.

By this time he seldom knew any of us who were about him, but took us all for strangers. This happened first with his sister, then with me, and finally with his servant. Such an alienation distressed me more than any other instance of his decay: though I knew that he had not really withdrawn his affection from me, yet his air and mode of addressing me gave me constantly that feeling. So much the more affecting was it, when the sanity of his perceptions and his remembrances returned; but these intervals were of slower and slower occurrence. In this condition, silent or babbling childishly, self-involved and torpidly abstracted, or else busy with self-created phantoms and delusions, what a contrast did he offer to *that* Kant who had once been the brilliant centre of the most brilliant circles for rank, wit, or knowledge, that Prussia afforded! A distinguished person from Berlin, who had called upon him during the preceding summer, was greatly shocked at his appearance, and said, 'This is not Kant that I have seen, but the shell of Kant!' How much more would he have said this, if he had seen him now!

Now came February, 1804, which was the last month that Kant was destined to see. It is remarkable that, in the memorandum book which I have before mentioned, I found a fragment of an old song, (inserted by Kant, and dated in the summer about six months before the time of his death,) which expressed that

February was the month in which people had the least weight to carry, for the obvious reason that it was shorter by two and by three days than the others; and the concluding sentiment was in a tone of fanciful pathos to this effect— 'Oh, happy February! in which man has least to bear—least pain, least sorrow, least self-reproach!' Even of this short month, however, Kant had not twelve entire days to bear; for it was on the 12th that he died; and in fact he may be said to have been dying from the 1st. He now barely vegetated; though there were still transitory gleams flashing by fits from the embers of his ancient intellect.

On the 3d of February the springs of life seemed to be ceasing from their play, for, from this day, strictly speaking, he ate nothing more. His existence henceforward seemed to be the mere prolongation of an impetus derived from an eighty years' life, after the moving power of the mechanism was withdrawn. His physician visited him every day at a particular hour; and it was settled that I should always be there to meet him. Nine days before his death, on paying his usual visit, the following little circumstance occurred, which affected us both, by recalling forcibly to our minds the ineradicable courtesy and goodness of Kant's nature. When the physician was announced, I went up to Kant and said to him, 'Here is Dr. A——.' Kant rose from his chair, and, offering his hand to the Doctor, murmured something in which the word 'posts' was frequently repeated, but with an air as though he wished to be helped out with the rest of the sentence. Dr. A——, who thought that, by *posts*, he meant the stations for relays of post-horses, and therefore that his mind was wandering, replied that all the horses were engaged, and begged him to compose himself. But Kant went on, with great effort to himself, and added—'Many posts, heavy posts—then much goodness—then much gratitude.' All this he said with apparent incoherence, but with great warmth, and increasing self-possession. I meantime perfectly divined what it was that Kant, under his cloud of imbecility, wished to say, and I interpreted accordingly. 'What the Professor wishes to say, Dr. A——, is this, that, considering the many and weighty offices which you fill in the city and in the university, it argues great goodness on your part to give up so much of your time to him,' (for Dr. A—— would never take any fees from Kant;) 'and that he has the deepest sense of this goodness.' 'Right,' said Kant, earnestly, 'right!' But he still continued to stand, and was nearly sinking to the ground. Upon which I remarked to the physician, that I was so well acquainted with Kant, that I was satisfied he would not sit down, however much he suffered from standing, until he knew that his visitors were seated. The Doctor seemed to doubt this—but Kant, who heard what I said, by a prodigious effort confirmed my construction of his conduct, and spoke distinctly these words —'God forbid I should be sunk so low as to forget the offices of humanity.'

When dinner was announced, Dr. A—— took his leave. Another guest had now arrived, and I was in hopes, from the animation which Kant had so recently displayed, that we should to-day have a pleasant party, but my hopes were vain—Kant was more than usually exhausted, and though he raised a spoon to his mouth, he swallowed nothing. For some time everything had been tasteless to him; and I had endeavored, but with little success, to stimulate the organs of taste by nutmeg, cinnamon, &c. To-day all failed, and I could not even prevail upon him to taste a biscuit, rusk, or anything of that sort. I had once heard him say that several of his friends, who had died of *marasmus*, had closed their illness by four or five days of entire freedom from pain, but totally without appetite, and then slumbered tranquilly away. Through this state I apprehended that he was himself now passing.

Saturday, the 4th of February, I heard his guests loudly expressing their fears that they should never meet him again; and I could not but share these fears myself. However, on Sunday, the 5th, I dined at his table in company with his particular friend Mr. R. R. V. Kant was still present, but so weak that his head drooped upon his knees, and he sank down against the right side of the chair. I went and arranged his pillows so as to raise and support his head; and, having done this, I said—'Now, my dear Sir, you are again in right order.' Great was our astonishment when he answered clearly and audibly in the Roman military phrase—'Yes, *testudine et facie*;' and immediately after added, 'Ready for the enemy, and in battle array.' His powers of mind were (if I may be allowed that expression) smouldering away in their ashes; but every now and then some lambent flame, or grand emanation of light, shot forth to make it evident that the ancient fire still slumbered below.

Monday, the 6th, he was much weaker and more torpid: he spoke not a word, except on the occasion of my question about the Moors, as previously stated, and sate with sightless eyes, lost in himself, and manifesting no sense of our presence, so that we had the feeling of some mighty shade or phantom from some forgotten century being seated amongst us.

About this time, Kant had become much more tranquil and composed. In the earlier periods of his illness, when his yet unbroken strength was brought into active contest with the first attacks of decay, he was apt to be peevish, and sometimes spoke roughly or even harshly to his servants. This, though very opposite to his natural disposition, was altogether excusable under the circumstances. He could not make himself understood: things were therefore brought to him continually which he had not asked for; and often it happened that what he really wanted he could not obtain, because all his efforts to name it were unintelligible. A violent nervous irritation, besides, affected him from the unsettling of the equilibrium in the different functions of his nature; weakness in one organ being made more palpable to him by disproportionate strength in another. But now the strife was over; the whole system was at length undermined, and in rapid and harmonious progress to dissolution. And from this time forward, no movement of impatience, or expression of fretfulness, ever escaped him.

I now visited him three times a-day; and on

Tuesday, Feb. 7th, going about dinner-time, I found the usual party of friends sitting down alone; for Kant was in bed. This was a new scene in his house, and increased our fears that his end was now at hand. However, having seen him rally so often, I would not run the risk of leaving him without a dinner-party for the next day; and accordingly, at the customary hour of one, we assembled in his house on

Wednesday, Feb. 8th. I paid my respects to him as cheerfully as possible, and ordered dinner to be served up. Kant sat at the table with us; and, taking a spoon with a little soup in it, put it to his lips; but immediately put it down again, and retired to bed, from which he never rose again, except during the few minutes when it was re-arranged.

Thursday, the 9th, he had sunk into the weakness of a dying person, and the corpse-like appearance had already taken possession of him. I visited him frequently through the day; and, going at ten o'clock at night, I found him in a state of insensibility. I could not draw any sign from him that he knew me, and I left him to the care of his sister and his servant.

Friday, the 10th, I went to see him at six o'clock in the morning. It was very stormy, and a deep snow had fallen in the night-time. And, by the way, I remember that a gang of house-breakers had forced their way through the premises in order to reach Kant's next neighbor, who was a goldsmith. As I drew near to his bed-side, I said, 'Good morning.' He returned my salutation by saying, 'Good morning,' but in so feeble and faltering a voice that it was hardly articulate. I was rejoiced to find him sensible, and I asked him if he knew me:—'Yes,' he replied; and, stretching out his hand, touched me gently upon the cheek. Through the rest of the day, whenever I visited him, he seemed to have relapsed into a state of insensibility.

Saturday, the 11th, he lay with fixed and rayless eyes; but to all appearance in perfect peace. I asked him again, on this day, if he knew me. He was speechless, but he turned his face towards me and made signs that I should kiss him. Deep emotion thrilled me, as I stooped down to kiss his pallid lips; for I knew that in this solemn act of tenderness he meant to express his thankfulness for our long friendship, and to signify his affection and his last farewell. I had never seen him confer this mark of his love upon anybody, except once, and that was a few weeks before his death, when he drew his sister to him and kissed her. The kiss which he now gave to me was the last memorial that he knew me.

Whatever fluid was now offered to him passed the oesophagus with a rattling sound, as often happens with dying people; and there were all the signs of death being close at hand.

I wished to stay with him till all was over; and as I had been witness of his life, to be witness also of his departure; and therefore I never quitted him except when I was called off for a few minutes to attend some private business. The whole of this night I spent at his bedside. Though he had passed the day in a state of insensibility, yet in the evening he made intelligible signs that he wished to have his bed put in order; he was therefore lifted out in our arms, and the bed-clothes and pillows being hastily arranged, he was carried back again. He did not sleep; and a spoonful of liquid, which was sometimes put to his lips, he usually pushed aside; but about one o'clock in the night he himself made a motion towards the spoon, from which I collected that he was thirsty; and I gave him a small quantity of wine and water sweetened; but the muscles of his mouth had not strength enough to retain it, so that to prevent its flowing back he raised his hand to his lips, until with a rattling sound it was swallowed. He seemed to wish for more; and I continued to give him more, until he said, in a way that I was just able to understand,—'It is enough.' And these were his last words. At intervals he pushed away the bed-clothes, and exposed his person; I constantly restored the clothes to their situation, and on one of these occasions I found that the whole body and extremities were already growing cold, and the pulse intermitting.

At a quarter after three o'clock on Sunday morning, February 12, Kant stretched himself out as if taking a position for his final act, and settled into the precise posture which he preserved to the moment of death. The pulse was now no longer perceptible to the touch in his hands, feet or neck. I tried every part where a pulse beats, and found none anywhere but in the left hip, where it beat with violence, but often intermitted.

About ten o'clock in the forenoon he suffered a remarkable change; his eye was rigid and his face and lips became discolored by a cadaverous pallor. Still, such was the effect of his previous habits, that no trace appeared of the cold sweat which naturally accompanies the last mortal agony.

It was near eleven o'clock when the moment of dissolution approached. His sister was standing at the foot of the bed, his sister's son at the head. I, for the purpose of still observing the fluctuations of the pulse in his hip, was kneeling at the bed-side; and I called his servant to come and witness the death of his good master. Now began the last agony, if to him it could be called an agony, where there seemed to be no struggle. And precisely at this moment, his distinguished friend, Mr. R. R. V., whom I had summoned by a messenger, entered the room. First of all, the breath grew feebler; then it missed its regularity of return; then it wholly intermitted, and the upper lip was slightly convulsed; after this there followed one slight respiration or sigh; and after that no more; but the pulse still beat for a few seconds—slower and fainter, till it ceased altogether; the mechanism stopped; the last motion was at an end; and exactly at that moment the clock struck eleven.

Soon after his death the head of Kant was shaved; and, under the direction of Professor Knorr, a plaster cast was taken, not a masque merely, but a cast of the whole bead, designed (I believe) to enrich the craniological collection of Dr. Gall.

The corpse being laid out and properly attired, immense numbers of people of every rank, from the highest to the lowest, flocked to see it. Everybody was anxious to make use of the last opportunity he would have for entitling himself to say—'I too have seen Kant.' This went on for many days —during which, from morning to night, the house was thronged with the public. Great was the astonishment of all people at the meagreness of Kant's appearance; and it was universally agreed that a corpse so wasted and fleshless had never been beheld. His head rested upon the same cushion on which once the gentlemen of the university had presented an address to him; and I thought that I could not apply it to a more honorable purpose than by placing it in the coffin, as the final pillow of that immortal head.

Upon the style and mode of his funeral, Kant had expressed his wishes in earlier years in a separate memorandum. He there desired that it should take place early in the morning, with as little noise and disturbance as possible, and attended only by a few of his most intimate friends. Happening to meet with this memorandum, whilst I was engaged at his request in arranging his papers, I very frankly gave him my opinion, that such an injunction would lay me, as the executor of his will, under great embarrassments; for that circumstances might very probably arise under which it would be next to impossible to carry it into effect. Upon this Kant tore the paper, and left the whole to my own discretion. The fact was, I foresaw that the students of the University would never allow themselves to be robbed of this occasion for expressing their veneration by a public funeral. The event showed that I was right; for a funeral such as Kant's, one so solemn and so magnificent, the city of Königsberg has never witnessed before or since. The public journals, and separate accounts in pamphlets, etc., have given so minute an account of its details, that I shall here notice only the heads of the ceremony.

On the 28th of February, at two o'clock in the afternoon, all the dignitaries of church and state, not only those resident in Königsberg, but from the remotest parts of Prussia, assembled in the church of the Castle. Hence they were escorted by the whole body of the University, splendidly dressed for the occasion, and by many military officers of rank, with whom Kant had always been a great favorite, to the house of the deceased Professor; from which the corpse was carried by torch-light, the bells of every church in Königsberg tolling, to the Cathedral which was lit up by innumerable wax- lights. A never-ending train of many thousand persons followed it on foot. In the Cathedral, after the usual burial rites, accompanied with every possible expression of national veneration to the deceased, there was a grand musical service, most admirably performed, at the close of which Kant's mortal remains were lowered into the academic vault, where he now rests among the ancient patriarchs of the University. PEACE BE TO HIS DUST, AND EVERLASTING HONOR!

---

1. By the paternal side, the family of Kant was of Scotch derivation; and hence it is that the name was written by Kant the father—*Cant*, that being a Scotch name, and still to be found in Scotland. But Immanuel, though he always cherished his Scotch descent, substituted a *K* for a *C*, in order to adapt it better to the analogies of the German language.
2. To this circumstance we must attribute its being so little known amongst the philosophers and mathematicians of foreign countries, and also the fact that D'Alembert, whose philosophy was miserably below

his mathematics, many years afterwards still continued to represent the dispute as a verbal one.

3. His reason for which was, that he considered the weather one of the principal forces which act upon the health; and his own frame was exquisitely sensible to all atmospheric influences.

4. To which the author should have added—and in regard to the hiatus between the planetary and cometary systems, which was pointed out by Kant several years before his conjecture was established by the good telescope of Dr. Herschel. Vesta and Juno, further confirmations of Kant's conjecture, were discovered in June 1804, when Wasianski wrote.

5. Mr. Wasianski is wrong. To pursue his meditations under these circumstances, might perhaps be an inclination of Kant's to which he yielded, but not one which he would justify or erect into a maxim. He disapproved of eating alone, or *solipsismus convictorii*, as he calls it, on the principle, that a man would be apt, if not called off by the business and pleasure of a social party, to think too much or too closely, an exercise which he considered very injurious to the stomach during the first process of digestion. On the same principle he disapproved of walking or riding alone; the double exercise of thinking and bodily agitation, carried on at the same time, being likely, as he conceived, to press too hard upon the stomach.

6. This appears less extraordinary, considering the description of Kant's person, given originally by Reichardt, about eight years after his death. 'Kant,' says this writer, 'was drier than dust both in body and mind. His person was small; and possibly a more meagre, arid, parched anatomy of a man, has not appeared upon this earth. The upper part of his face was

grand; forehead lofty and serene, nose elegantly turned, eyes brilliant and penetrating; but below it expressed powerfully the coarsest sensuality, which in him displayed itself by immoderate addiction to eating and drinking.' This last feature of his temperament is here expressed much too harshly.

7. This theory was afterwards greatly modified in Germany; and, judging from the random glances which I throw on these subjects, I believe that in this recast it still keeps its ground in that country.

8. Mr. Wasianski is quite in the wrong here. If the hindrances which nature presented to the act of thinking were now on the increase, on the other hand, the disposition to think, by his own acknowledgment, was on the wane. The power and the habit altering in proportion, there is no case made out of that disturbed equilibrium to which apparently he would attribute the headaches. But the fact is, that, if he had been as well acquainted with Kant's writings as with Kant personally, he would have known, that some affection of the head of a spasmodic kind was complained of by Kant at a time when nobody could suspect him of being in a decaying state.

9. How this happened to be the case in Germany, Mr. Wasianski has not explained. Perhaps the English merchants at Königsberg, being amongst Kant's oldest and most intimate friends, had early familiarized him to the practice of drinking tea, and to other English tastes. However, Jachmann tells us, (p. 164,) that Kant was extravagantly fond of coffee, but forced himself to abstain from it under a notion that it was very unwholesome.

10. Wasianski here returns thanks to some unknown person, who, having observed that Kant in his latter walks took pleasure in leaning against a particular

wall to view the prospect, had caused a seat to be fixed at that point for his use.

11. Mr. Wasianski says—*late* in summer: but, as he elsewhere describes by the same expression of 'late in summer,' a day which was confessedly *before* the longest day, and as the multitude of birds which continued to sing will not allow us to suppose that the summer could be very far advanced, I have translated accordingly.

12. For Kant's particular complaint, as described by other biographers, a quarter of a grain of opium, every twelve hours, would have been the best remedy, perhaps a perfect remedy.

13. Who these worthy people were that criticised Kant's eating, is not mentioned. They could have had no opportunity of exercising their abilities on this question, except as hosts, guests, or fellow-guests; and in any of those characters, a gentleman, one would suppose, must feel himself degraded by directing his attention to a point of that nature. However, the merits of the case stand thus between the parlies: Kant, it is agreed by all his biographers, ate only once a day; for as to his breakfast, it was nothing more than a very weak infusion of tea, (vide Jachmann's Letters, p. 163,) with no bread, or eatable of any kind. Now, his critics, by general confession, ate their way, from 'morn to dewy eve,' through the following course of meals: 1. Breakfast early in the morning; 2. Breakfast *à la fourchette* about ten, A.M.; 3. Dinner at one or two; 4. Vesper Brod; 5. Abend Brod; all which does really seem a very fair allowance for a man who means to lecture upon abstinence at night. But I shall cut this matter short by stating one plain fact; there were two things, and no more, for which Kant had an inordinate craving during his whole life; these were tobacco and

coffee; and from both these he abstained almost altogether, merely under a sense of duty, resting probably upon erroneous grounds. Of the first he allowed himself a very small quantity, (and everybody knows that temperance is a more difficult virtue than abstinence;) of the other none at all, until the labors of his life were accomplished.

14. In this, as in many other things, the taste of Kant was entirely English and Roman; as, on the other hand, some eminent Englishmen, I am sorry to say, have, on this very point, shown the effeminacy and *falsetto* taste of the Germans. In particular, Mr. Coleridge, describing, in The Friend, the custom amongst German children of making presents to their parents on Christmas Eve, (a custom which he unaccountably supposes to be peculiar to Ratzeburg,) represents the mother as 'weeping aloud for joy'—the old idiot of a father with 'tears running down his face,' &c. &c., and all for what? For a snuff-box, a pencil-case, or some article of jewellery. Now, we English agree with Kant on such maudlin display of stage sentimentality, and are prone to suspect that papa's tears are the product of rum-punch. Tenderness let us have by all means, and the deepest you can imagine, but upon proportionate occasions, and with causes fitted to justify it and sustain its dignity.

15. To whom it appears that Kant would generally reply, upon their expressing the pleasure it gave them to see him, 'In me you behold a poor superannuated, weak, old man.'

16. Mr. W. here falls into the ordinary mistake of confounding the cause and the occasion, and would leave the impression, that Kant (who from his youth up had been a model of temperance) died of sensual indulgence. The cause of Kant's death was clearly the

general decay of the vital powers, and in particular the atony of the digestive organs, which must soon have destroyed him under any care or abstinence whatever. This was the cause. The accidental occasion, which made that cause operative on the 7th of October, might or might not be what Mr. W. says. But in Kant's burthensome state of existence, it could not be a question of much importance whether his illness were to commence in an October or a November.

17. *Physical* Geography, in opposition to *Political*.